For my children

Don, Mariama, Laini, Bomani, Akili

In Memory of

Henry Blakely II
Walter Bradford
Michael Dorris
Curt Flood
Leon Forrest
Murray Kempton
Queen Mother Moore
John H. Sengstacke
Ann Petry
Betty Shabazz
Coleman Young

Acknowledgements

To the students, faculty, staff and administration at Chicago State University my intellectual home and the residence of the Gwendolyn Brooks Center for Creative Writing and Black Literature. To my editors at Third World Press Gwendolyn Mitchell and Melissa Moore and, of course, my family Safisha, Inez, Laini, Bomani and Akili, Gwendolyn Brooks, Drake Thomas and Juanita Rayner.

HeartLove

Books by Haki R. Madhubuti

Claiming Earth: Race, Rage, Rape, Redemption: Blacks Seeking a Culture of Enlightened Empowerment

Dynamite Voices: Black Poets of the 1960's

Black Men: Obsolete, Single Dangerous? The Afrikan American Family in Transition

From Plan to Planet: Life Studies: The Need for Afrikan Minds and Institutions

Enemies: The Clash of Races

A Capsule Course in Black Poetry Writing (co-authored with Gwendolyn Brooks, Keorapetse Kgositsile and Dudley Randall)

Poetry

Groundwork: New and Selected Poems of Don L. Lee/Haki R. Madhubuti from 1966–1996

Killing Memory, Seeking Ancestors

Earthquakes and Sunrise Missions

Book of Life

Directionscore: New and Selected Poems

We Walk the Way of the New World

Don't Cry, Scream

Black Pride

Think Black

Anthologies

Million Man March/Day of Absence: A Commemorative Anthology: Speeches, Commentary, Photography, Poetry, Illustrations and Documents (co-edited by Maulana Karenga)

Confusion by Any Other Name: Essays Exploring the Negative Impact of the Blackman's Guide to Understanding the Blackwoman

Why L.A. Happened: Implications of the '92 Los Angeles Rebellion

Say That the River Turns: The Impact of Gwendolyn Brooks

To Gwen, With Love (co-edited with Pat Brown and Francis Ward)

HeartLove
Wedding and Love Poems

Haki R. Madhubuti

Artwork by Jon Onye Lockard

THIRD WORLD PRESS   Chicago

Third World Press
Publishers Since 1967
Chicago

Printed in the United States of America

04 03 02 01 00 99
 5 4 3 2 1

Cover and inside illustrations by Jon Onye Lockard
Cover design by Nicole M. Mitchell

Library of Congress Cataloging-in-Publication Data

Madhubuti, Haki R., 1942-
    HeartLove: wedding, love, and extended family poems / by
Haki R. Madhubuti
    p. cm.

    ISBN: 0-88378-201-4 (pbk.)
    1. Afro-American—Poetry. I. Title.
PS3563.A3397H43 1998
811' .54—dc21

                                                    98-15418
                                                         CIP

A number of these poems were previously published in *Killing
Memory, Seeking Ancestors, Book of Life, Black Men, Earthquakes and
Sunrise Missions,* and *GroundWork.* Other selections appeared in the
following publications: *Essence, The Source, Emerge, Warpland,
Tamaqua, Fertile Ground,* and *In Search of Color Everywhere.*

Contents

Extended Families

Maintaining Loveships

There are many paragraphs in a life of love. I say "paragraph" because the stanza of poetry is still foreign to most of us. Love is a living river running slowly north to south, traversing the entire human continent. Love is like the Mississippi River experiencing all types of weather, hot to cold, warm to cool, frigid to steaming hot. Find the weather of the person you love, monitor it often. Or like the river's weather, adjust your body temperatures to accommodate the other in your life and adapt to your own definitions of happiness, stability, and seriousness. Remember that love is not a swimming contest, and most of us will never learn to backstroke. Learn to swim upstream together.

Bonding—mating, and preferably marriage to another—is or can be music. (Much of the time, in this culture, it is regrettable noise.) However, this bonding can be the best of the early Supremes, Miracles, Four Tops and Nat King Cole. Some of us measured our early happiness with each new cut by the Dells: "Stay in My Corner." Coupling is also Bessie Smith, Billie Holiday and, yes, Nina Simone—as they sing with tears in their eyes, "Am I Blue?" We choose our dancing partners. We can either two-step, tap, do modern, African, the breakdown, or get in line and pulse. Whatever tune we choose will demand work, require navigating the personal river of the other, require the sharing of the most intimate spaces. We may be southern in our spirit, yet, too often, our struggle is to neutralize the northern winds blowing ice into our lives. Think in bright possibilities.

To the Men

Women are different in so many beautiful ways. I wonder if we men really ever sit down within our own questions and ponder the complicated melodies of the woman/women in our lives? Do we ever try to put our feet and souls into their shoes and spirits? Each woman is her own color, is her own stream, is her own season, and has her own personal weather report. We must listen to our women. We must know the winds of our women. Often these winds come with hurricane force, but mostly they arrive smoothly so as not to take either of us off center. The women in our lives are the balances that keep our families from falling too far off course. If there is to be "war," let it be against superficial assessments of women. Do not fear intelligent, self-reliant, independent, strong-willed, and culturally focused women. Seek them. Most of these women have strong backs, questions and answers. They harbor ships of love. They also hold within them the pain and happiness of large families and culturally defined histories. The most serious of them think in long distance and careful sentences. If they are with children, they function always with a clock in them. Most of them carry the pulse of their children close to their hearts. They also carry the smiles of the men they love tightly in the vicinity of the same heart. We must begin to carry the spirits of our women in us. We must open our mind's eye to the great possibilities that serious mating represents for our future. This is HeartLove.

To the Women

Men are beautiful in so many different ways. They come
with unorganized heartbeats. They come, often ready to learn,
ready to be taught a different rhythm. Like their toes, the size
and shape of their hearts are hiding complicated fears. Young
men fear women. They hide their fears in muted language and
quiet cool. At dances, they hold up walls with their backs, a
mean lean carefully shaped to give off messages of "I'm
ready." Generally with one or more of their brothers they sig-
nal that, "We're ready." "Ready for what?" is the question. Too
many men function overtime in ways to impress other men,
mainly their fathers or mentors, brothers, uncles, grandfathers,
teachers, or coaches. They buy into the "impressions" business
too early. Often the men talk in codes. Men do not beat
around the bush, men beat the bush. Most men do not talk or
sing to the woman/women in their lives the music that is pul-
sating in their minds. We think that we are lovers, or we want
to be lovers, but seldom contemplate the meaning of love. Too
many of us have been taught "love" by our peers and the
street. Too often this is translated into the physical only.
Women represent children, commitment, sharing, and long-dis-
tance conversations about tomorrows and fears. But, we do
not listen. Too many men come ill-prepared for love, for shar-
ing, for deep-river rides, having spent too much time in the
northern hemisphere of their minds. Men need understand-
ing, good instructions, and magic in their lives. Women repre-
sent all of this to us. This is HeartLove.

To the Men and Women

Marriage, mating or bonding is not a vacation or a prolonged holiday. Eighty percent of a marriage is work, compromise, adaptations, changes, intimate conversations, laughter, sexual sharing, confusion, joy, smiles, tears, pain, crises, re-education, community, apologies, mistakes, more mistakes, new knowledge, and love. If children are involved, include parenting and repeat everything above twice for each year of the marriage. If the marriage lasts more than fifteen years, the couple should add wisdom and many, many thank-yous. What about the other twenty percent? I presume that even in the most successful marriages, the couples will sleep.

Remember, the deepest hurt is the hurt inflicted by lovers. To remain lovers is hard work; it is not natural. Mating/marriage is cultural. Most things grow old. The key to beautiful tomorrows is involvement in a loveship that ages gracefully. We are bound to make mistakes in our loveships, but the lesson is to learn and grow from them. Always listen to your mistakes, learn from your mistakes.

If Black women do not love, there is no love. As the women go, so go the people. Stopping the woman stops the future. If Black women do not love, strength disconnects, families sicken, growth is questionable, and there are few reasons to conquer ideas or foes. If Black men do not love, shouting starts, the shooting commences, boys fill prisons, and our women grow gardens off to themselves. If Black women and men love, so come flowers from sun, rainbows at dusk. As Black women and men connect, the earth expands, minds open and our yeses become natural as we seek HeartLove.

Wedding Poems

The Union of Two

For Ife and Jacob Carruthers
August 7, 1986

what matters is the renewing and long running kinship
seeking common mission, willing work, memory,
   melody, song.

marriage is an art,
created by the serious, enjoyed by the mature,
watered with morning and evening promises.

those who grow into love
remain anchored
like egyptian architecture and seasonal flowers

it is african that woman and man join in smile, tears,
       future.
it is traditional that men and women share
       expectations, celebrations, struggles.
it is legend that the nations start in the family.
it is african that our circle expands.
it is wise that we believe in tomorrows, children, quality.
it is written that our vision will equal the promise.

so that your nation will live and tell your stories accurately.
you must be endless in your loving touch of each other.
your unification is the message,
continuance the answer.

A Bonding

For Susan Taylor and Khephra Burns
August 20, 1989

we were forest people,
landrooted, vegetable strong.
feet fastened to soil with earth strengthened toes.
determined fruit,
anchored
where music soared,
where dancers circled,
where writers sang,
where griots gave memory,
where smiles were not bought.

you have come to each other in wilderness,
in this time of cracked concrete, diminished vision,
    wounded rain.

at the center of flowers your craft is on fire.
only ask for what you can give.

do not forget bright mornings, hands touching
under moonlight, filtered water for your plants,
healing laughter, renewing futures. caring.

your search has been rewarded, marriage is not
logical, it's necessary. we have a way of running
yellow lights, it is now that we must claim
the sun in our hearts. your joining is a mending, a quilt.

as determined fruit
you have come late to the music.
only ask for what you can give.
you have asked for each other.

DarkRooted: The Joining

For Marilyn and David Hall
June 23, 1990

it is said each morning before parting, before meeting
the wind, the two of you clasp suntouched hands &
sing a quiet prayer for the continued wholeness & safety
of the other. anchoring. it is known that your four hands
touching softly complete the first circle, mending
the two of you quilt-like into an unending image of
      long-distances
earth trees. in this kente-cloth man who is brother to
his community lies deep well values, wind-swept valleys.
mountains. broad memory, historical pain, committed
joy. energy. determined force. i've seen his father.
in this batik-cloth woman whose beauty graced our eyes
there is crystal-hope. renewing grass spirit, watered fruit,
heartbeat cool, active brain, willing searcher.
serious runner. i've seen the people of her homeland.
we listen to the sunlight burning between your hearts.
we confirm the enchanted beat of your calling.
as in water conversing with sea rocks we come
      touch-tongue,
we come joyfully to your circle,
duplicating the quest. you are yes. anchored african trees.
darkrooted. ones.

Answers: This Magic Moment

For Gina and Chester
August 18, 1990

now that you have young love
insist upon the dawn,
its mornings bright with sun and rain
that summon up continuity.

now that your love is bonded and
culturally confirmed, do not forget:
first meetings, great and early laughter,
preparation for first dates, delicate touches and
kisses that quicken heartbeats, love notes and
phone calls into the midnights' dawns. do not forget
promises; there are always pure promises of,
        "forever yours."

now that you are one and one. matched.
remember the path that joined you.

now that you have traditional clarity and
are blessed with conscientious givers among you,
do not forget world without light or hope,
do not forget brutality, hunger, raw violence
visited upon children.

share the beauty in your eyes this day,
grow into mature love, leaving little for granted.

insist upon the dawn,
its mornings bright with sun and rain,
summoning rainbows and continuity,
summoning you here. brilliantly beautiful,
caring, content, young lovers,
growing into your promises,
confirming life,
confirming us,
giving an answer.

Breathing the Breadth of the Other

For Lynn and Ron Rochon
August 22, 1993

same love different decades.
we've seen the sun
rise
melting loud promises of our twenties.
the young do not love carefully,
the young innocently love, often,
the young *live* with wishes of no boredom.

you are mature young
a decade past romanticism,
years on the other side of searching,
months away from intimate hunger,
weeks from assigning blame,
days removed from contemplating advice from
   relatives,
within seconds confirming, we are ready!

these are your commitments:

a. listen first, listen last, communicate
b. when angry, hit the couch in private instead of each
   other.
c. measure each other's pulse seven times a week; do
   not buy a pulse meter.
d. divide the housework
     B.C. (Before Children)

       you[1]: garbage, dishes, bedroom, car, kitchen,
            mopping, weekly wash, cooking, shopping,
            no pets.

       you[2]: living room, bathroom, halls, cooking, car,
            sweeping, shopping, weekly wash, kitchen,
            argue for a cat.

A.C. (After Children) revise everything

e. encourage growth in each other. intelligence may
   marry stupid, but brains don't stay with pinheads.

f. parent against the culture; if you spend $100 on
   Nintendo, your children will become what you
   deserve.

g. do not take current beauty for granted. big eaters
   are wrong. fat is not pretty nor healthy.

h. grow into greater love, nothing stays the same.
   challenge the beauty in each other. fight for
   understanding.

we've seen the sun
rise
in you
knowing the bones in her back,
feeling the tenderness of his feet,

same love, different decade,
breathing the scent of each other
breath to breath
sustaining the music of bright expectations
life comfirmed. complete.
one.

Long Distance Lovers

Long distance lovers are those
who against the laughter
of doubts and anti-commitments
have hung tough
in a
civilization of perpetual partings
and wounded children

Quiet Mountains to Your Elegance
For Carolyn and Charles on 25 years of marriage
September 19, 1993

Yours is a regenerative descant.

This community has witnessed your maturation,
this community has participated in the birth and
   nurturing of your child,
this community has embraced your design,
this community has grown in the glow of your
   commitment.

Now that you have chosen to rejoice
in this quarter century of your love
we too renew our song.

We grow quiet mountains to your elegance.
yours are right memory, precious culture,
intricate calling, bonding,
affirming the Africa reach in us.
The exactness of your love replenishes the drumbeat in
   our steps.
Come as calm weather, muted in the understanding
that within decades of tumultuous stirrings
your melody is original antique,
determined answering, a smile.

Let this be our legacy,
our melody.

Translations

For Gerry and John Howell
August 27, 1994

She has unearthed your center
it is attached to the heart of
this woman.
does she know your history,
has she deciphered your language,
has she made any sense of your diet,
does your reading of books frighten her?

Does she know that you have brothers
with different last names?

You come to the union as experienced practitioners
pained, gutted, illuminated, with children,
cleansed, wiser.

She will bring balance to your life.
What will you give her?

Try the promise of loving longevity
consultant happiness,
measured music of the Dells and Four Tops
indigenous beauty,
try the abandonment of weakening habits.

There are mountains in the two of you
climb each other regularly
watch for mudslides and cracks in the rocks.
Your life-line is love and
intimate distance spaced by
silent yeses confirming
"this magic moment so different and so new"
your voices,
perfectly pitched, natural.
Sing your songs.

Contemplating Full Orchards

For Bakari Kitwana and Monique Jacques
November 26, 1995

New York City is not a place to watch
the sun or grow a forest. agreed.

I speak from the tongue of a father,
a brother, as one who has known deep love.

This marriage is not an exam. You are now
entering the rooms of living mysteries where
prophesy reveals itself as knowledge and mother-wit.
this is the clearest contingency for love:
      commitment to differences, listening, compromise,
      assigned prescriptive silences,
      learned laughter, artful music and essential values.

in fresh marriages you are exposed
like new seeds in earth,
like delinquent gossip from children,
like well water to the earth's organisms.
define your memories gracefully.

sweet, sweet lovers
crowd your bed in each other.
rise each day with distinctive voices
contemplating full orchards draped in
bountiful moons of mastered touching,
accepting unpredictables,
expecting well-placed joy. agreed.

Memories are Made for Poets

For Sharon Franklin Taylor and Useni Eugene Perkins
November 30, 1996

in our adolescence we played at love
the kind that surfaced for too many pretty faces
attached to bodies that stopped one's breath   always
surrounded by innocent laughter that continued
until the rings were firmly placed
on the left side of our hearts.

memories are made of this.

in this season of ripened watermelons,
pre-driven cars and year-round vegetables from
   California
we now accept breathless prayers
while gently exchanging thread, bread and long life
with this elegant woman who knows God and you.
she believes you are the river running into her desert.
we are here to confirm the richness of her earth,
of her decision.

the truth is that this poet does not wish to age alone
and is known by many and most
to recognize succint beauty and deep love
especially if such love is shining luminously upon him.

The Reconstitution of
all their Days and Nights

For Benard King and Nequai Taylor
August 23, 1997

are the lovers
soon to be husband and wife
ready to ride their words and deeds of obligation?
have they been schooled in the art of long nights
in and out of each other's arms?
have they tasted the bittersweet days of doubt and boredom?
what of the great possibility of children, yes
children with exposed hearts and innocent eyes
demanding the reconstitution of all of their days and
        nights, forthcoming?

tell them loudly that the love of each other is not enough!
that knowing, that family, that towering expectations,
that community steeped in luminous tradition
coupled with the laws and lows of deep valleys
harboring the necessity of memory, meaning and
touch all reaching
for the perfection of new days as promised in muted signs
only if they listen and love, do mindful work
        and love, speak good words
        and love, share meaningful values
        and love, grow into each other responsibly
        and love,   to love deeply like earthmusic dancing
life from the drums of our dreams, beating rough water,
beating ripe wind, beating bright sun,
drumming these young hearts into family.

The Preparation Chant

(minister)

in the hollow night the bells ring,
in the basement under dim lights the bellmaker sings,
in the closet, in the house across from the church the
      minister makes ready,
in the hot breath of a child, the sister to the bride,
      a smile is seen,
in the mixed steps of the brother to the groom
      a dance is forming,
in the words of the father we are here in love and love,
in the actions of the mother seen at 6:00 a.m. running
      into the church,
in the questions asked by children waiting to eat,
in the mission of *this* man and *this* woman memorizing
      their commitments,
in the quiet of their community contemplating
      a party, quilt and prodigy.

(bride and groom)

Wait:
on this occasion of pure water, rain, river runs,
lakefront beauty, waterfalls, dreams of warm baths,
it is the right clean,
the telling of our stories, the ocean of Black memory that must
be underpenned, strengthened, made holy, praised, stretched
higher than the expected.
the two is one. sun filled prerequisite for family,
for future, for accepting secrets reserved for careful, careful
lovers. we join the community.
open eyed, deeply considered having studied *the* texts
and listened to our elders.

(maid of honor)

Why:
it is observed, some say that it is written,
others talk of permanency and the need for quality
reproduction. nonaccidental births.
refreshing music, history understood,
a politics of mutual respect in a society of knowers,
builders, artists, musicians, writers, poets, teachers,
pastors, chiropractors, herbalists and
volunteer gardeners who teach that farming is
fundamental to civilization.
producing can-do people not afraid of kindness or
melody or sweet yeses.

(best man)

Start:
before the introductions, before the knowledge of God,
before the attraction of opposites,
before the melting of hearts,
before the empty sidewalks intersect your centers.
define your common music, construct a future
into right-propositions, proposals, preparations and expecta-
tions. kneel to a quality life with a person better than you are,
rise sweet summer,
rise with the wisdom of grandmothers,
rise understanding that creation is on-going,
immensely appealing and acceptable to fools
and geniuses, and those of us in between.

(minister)

in the coming day light,
in the willful act of sharing bed and fruit,
in the commitment of supreme sacrifices for the couple's good,
in accepting the carelessness and ignorance of youth
    and past lives,
in the first questions of survival, sameness and civility,
in the promises of deep passion, pasture, passage and work,
in the activism of protecting culture, people,
    ideas and clean water,
in the spirit of that which is greater than we are allowed
    to know or be,
in the privacy of two people who have exchanged
    wood, fire, earth and pancakes,
in the oneness of shared hearts acknowledging responsibility,
holy words and family.

(bride and groom)

we now carry each others bags, histories, vegetables, dreams,
common concerns, furniture
and end each others sentences with more periods
than question marks.
as we make our house sacred,
prosperous, complimentary and joyous.

Quality of Love

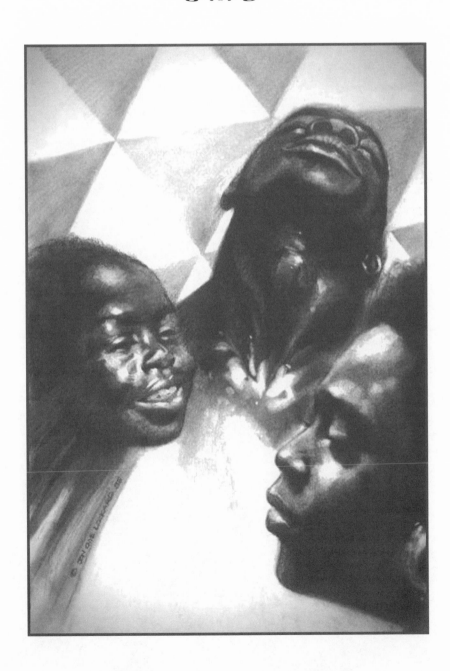

The Only Time

the only time a man
can tell a woman
he loved her too much is when
he doesn't mean it.

Love Gets Too Much Credit
Until It Finds You

you don't find love it finds you
not that love is hidden or unavailable
it's on its own mission searching for receptive souls.
love cannot be bought, sold or ordered with dinner,
cannot be charged on gold cards or revolving accounts,
cannot be bartered with food stamps, coupons or promises,
cannot be redeemed with cashier checks or money orders.
love is seasoned and concealed in fine fire,
delicate music and accessible secrets that are quilted
to the tone of distinctive voices wrapped in unconditions and
clear commitments
created for unique lovers who have matured
and are prepared to receive the most precious of stones
allowing love to tango its cultured language generously
and unencumbered into the essence of those
who are blessed.

Tough Love

his soul knows no calling,
hears few kind footsteps.
he talks street & prison with right hand on his privates,
his pants hang low on his hip bone,
his language is protective & guttural,
he sees with one eye,
his walk is drum-dance,
he runs with the roughroad tribe,
wears black glove on left fist.
has never known a personal smile from an adult,
his knowledge is popular, urban & short.
he discovered moon, sun & flowers at 20,
the elder in his life is 26 and like him
knows he is in trouble.
he's seeking a distant memory, a calling

last week a smiling woman called his name,
she wasn't carrying weeds or guns or junk food.

She Never Grew Up

She lost herself in *people* magazine beauty.
family and strangers started telling her
how beautiful she was before she was born
she absorbed their words at birth & never let go.

her color is mango black wrapped around innocent
green eyes.
she had a smile that was invented for her teeth.
the beauty confirming words clouded her memory
and impeded her walk.
she had deficient family to protect her.
at 29 she was an old woman.
men had given her everything that
she & they thought she needed.
they stole her youth
unmarried with 8 children
she didn't know the intimate history of her lovers
they all told her, repeatedly
how beautiful she was.

the color of mango black with green eyes
she could not see the lies from men who
always swore that they deeply loved her just before
they parted her legs,
rode her like a horse,
took her juice
left their seed &
never said good-bye.

Why She Loves Him

she seldom would admit to him the reasons she was
attracted his way (not necessarily in this order):
looks, hair, tone of voice, content of his conversation, body
scent, his infectious smile,
manners, kindness & ideas. the drape of his clothes,
the quietness of his intentions & interior, care for
others, the questions he asked,
his understanding of multiple realities, his culture &
politics, his insistence upon paying for dinner,
movies & music while dating.
he is unpredictable, well traveled with a large
mind & is unpretentious. the way he smiles
at children & gravitates toward them,
his advocacy of extended family, love of exercise,
walking, love of land.
he doesn't smoke, drink, do drugs or sleep around,
does not think it right, necessary or safe to have sex
on the first, second, third or fourth dates,
he feels that birth control is his responsibility too, clean, loves
to visit bookstores, libraries, farms,
museums and art galleries, read books,
quarterlies and magazines that have more text than
pictures. adores visual art, music, movies and theater.
respectful of women's dreams and vision.
he doesn't eat meat, fish, chicken or dairy products.
productive and economically independent,
not jealous, mentally and physically sound,
an intense caring lover and yoga practitioner. the
spiritualness of his utterances and
his presence quiets her.
the way he communicates without words is precious, and
she knows the exact location of his heart.

Rainforest

you are forest   rain
dense with life green colors
forever pulling the blue of life into you
see you walk and
i would burst rainwater into you
swim in & out of you
opening you like anxious earthquakes
uncontrollable but beautiful & dangerous.

get with this woman   come
fire frozen beauty,
men cannot sleep around you
your presence demands attention
demands notice
demands touch & motion & communication.

you are runner
swift like warm hurricanes
fast like stolen firebirds
& you disrupt the silence in me
make me speak memories forgotten & unshared.
secrets uttered in strange storms,
deep full sounds reserved for magical,
magical lovers.

listen runner
i have shared pain with you,
i have commented on future worlds to you,
i have let you touch the weak & strong of me,
i have tasted the tip of your ripeness &
kissed sweat from your middle.

i have bit into your mouth and
sucked the lifeforces from your insides   and
i know you. understand you.
i have shared books and travel and music and
growth with you

sweet knows honey & i know you.
under salted water tides
& running against polluted earth
i've tried to be good to you woman
tried to care beyond words
          care beyond distant spaces
sensitive phases & quiet lies
care
beyond cruel music & false images.

you are original high & dream maker
& true men do not try to limit you.

listen woman black
i do not wish to dominate your dreams
or obstruct your vision.
trust my motion   feel
know that i am near & with you
& will cut the cold of winter winds to reach you.
you
are delicate bronze
in spring-summers & special autumns
you are   forest rain
dark & runner & hurricane-black
frequently
i say frequently i bring you
midnight   *rain*.

Laini

nurtured like her mother
wondrous,
contemplative & self absorbed.
she assigned herself a capacious journey.
new york city is a frightening certainty.
i cried when she returned
whole & enlarged & well.
still avoiding vegetables & housework.

For Mariama
Spelman Commencement
May 22, 1995

The sun has blessed you.
this ritual of light,
this necessary coming out,
this gathering of sisters, mothers, grandmothers,
this awakening,
this journey,
this deciding step,
this quality walk,
this gathering of family, extended family, people,
this welcoming rootedness,
this earth warming call,
this Black high jump,
this continuation of Leslie, Alfre, Alice, and Johnnetta,*
this double-dutch of ready-women,
this calm before the *yes*,
this Africa across the seas,
you are our deep calculation,
embrace your numbers
come to this moment,
run to the new century without apology or slowness.
you are affirmation and clean-sound
mind your wealth internally and
never forget your name.

*Leslie Richards, Alfre Woodard, Alice Walker, and Johnnetta B. Cole

In Our Tradition

(for the brothers)

his woman is sitting on the back porch,
insects feed off the sweat of her lean body,
they have just finished making love.
she hurried out of the room
to cry
away from his smiles & smell.
after the flood of '95
she had promised herself that before
she loved him again
she would take to the fields, break bread with nuns
look wolves in the eye & kneel before the sea of light
to armor her heart away from his touch.

her breath young & spirited,
her eyes lucent & unequivocal
betrayed the armor about her heart

it is he who promised her heartlove
it is she who questions the love in
his heart.

Alone Much Of The Time

The women he experienced and enjoyed life with
were fine, intelligent, children loving & smiled naturally.
Most were intuitive, self-starters & understood balance.
he avoided women with multicolored finger nails,
all the answers,
processed or finger waved hair styles,
smokers, drinkers, excessive talkers,
soap opera & talk show enthusiasts while
side stepping women who wore clothes
glued to their bodies like balloons to air.
he didn't care for gossipers, nonreaders, big
eaters or women who were cultureless
and believed that the only use for money is to spend it.

What Makes Him Happy

this woman who loves black & white photographs is
brightfaced, blessed with deep-rooted & perspicuous eyes,
carries one hundred & thirty-five pounds of tall,
lean beauty draped on African bones uses
liquid soap that smells of peppermint or almond;
drives her car barefooted.

she appreciates the difficult differences
between Toni Morrison and William Faulkner,
understands that the free market is really a family affair,
has tasted and lost profound love and experienced
the pain and miracle of giving birth.
this woman runs a mile in under nine minutes
and believes that billie holiday, john coltrane &
louis armstrong are alive & still swingin, says
she loves vegetables, brown rice, nectarines & her son.

she relaxes with films that need subtitles,
music that requires a mind and her man
who is comfortable with complexity and enchantment.
she is contemplative about romare bearden's signature
        on his paintings,
& has a smile that evokes volcanoes in men.
she has god in her heart but doesn't brag about it,
prefers baths to showers & sweetens her body with
        olive/aloe oil.

her home is art-full as are the five rings decorating her
        fingers & ears
her hair which she cuts herself, is shaped close to her head
she has a museum of a memory & articulates her love and
thoughts firmly & passionately while listening to
billie, trane & pops collaborating
in black & blue eight-scale harmonies,
the music, the traditions & the way of our tomorrows.

Risk Everything

I

at thirty-six you had tasted and tested life.
it had not conformed or confused you.
you could count your losses and loves on either hand,
a slow count. one love for each decade minus the first. in your
twenties you were blessed with a son with a man who had
detoured to a corner of your heart
without experiencing sun, healing
water or the voices of enlightened ancestors.
you traveled south and birthed a boy genius. this is to say you
always total your journey, could read a map at night and were
never without cab fare. your mother taught you her pain and
laughter, your
grandmother said,"men needed excuses." your father proved
her correct. your aunts schooled you in the lies of women. it
was left to you to
locate the intimate and intricate truths. your best girl
friend taught you how to fix
cars that you drove as if your soul was glued to the steering
wheel of better destinations.

you found that men were like unchartered continents
most are undeveloped nations,
often tribal in their limitations,
too many unable to reach their own knowledges
or questions. having your own son to raise,
you refuse to suffer for boys in grown folks clothes.
in your fourth decade you allow a man into your life who was
not looking for you.
he spoke in poems and strange food.
he looked at you for a full year before he said yes.
he realized that you were a compass, a liberated zone, careful
and sure. discriminating. lean with love.

II

you take my ebony stone and i take yours.
breathe on it, touch it to your heart. like stones we
are not new to earth or love, we've planted seeds at
    midnight.
we approach the sun cleansed. whole. awaken to
    shape a memory.
no longer young young our expectations are like the
    stones:
hard melody, created-in sweet heat.
    everlasting. focused.
shaped in deep histories by the unimpressionable
medications of struggle and deep rooted greens.
we are the fundamental witness to each other's
requirements. supportive and thankful.
these stones are not to be cast away. ever.
they carry spirited devotion and tender joy
they are our markings and maps,
they are our delicate signatures.

Often Hard to Believe
For my sons Don, Bomani & Akili

there are thinking, loving, giving, good & kind men
among us. there are men who consider others first &
more, who are secure,
generous, well adjusted, liberated, competitive,
competent & contemplative. around us are creative,
talented & confident, big eaters & men who fast.
in our communities are children caring, women caring
& loving, partying, intuitive, hard working & joyous
men occupying the frozen memory of all. within these grounds
are men who cook, clean, build & marry.
resourceful, peaceful, peace loving & peace giving men toil the
earth together.
on their knees are spiritual, meditative, deep thinking &
praying brothers.
gathered musically here are healthy, sportsminded,
sexually sensitive, strong,
profoundly loving & cultural men
who understand & practice reciprocity.
they know the hurt, hearts & missions of women,
they feel the bones, secrets & hearts of men,
they anticipate, defend & nurture the innocence in
    children.
in their psychology are defiant warriors existing between
turbulence & honor.
seldom highlighted are the bold men who articulate & carry
the fears of others.
among men are dreamers, doers & doubters who will not

betray a trust.
they are fathers & parents who love so deeply that they are
often misunderstood.
in their quietness is patience, calmness & forbearance that
some read as weakness,
impotence & vulnerability.
in all of this they naturally smile & occasionally
belly-laugh.
these beauty-seekers safeguard civilization & we need to be
reminded of their open-hearted presence in
abundance among us.
often & more they run against the accepted &
encourage definitions of ignorant hard hats, drunken soldiers,
arrogant professors & immature politicians
who swim in egocentric heat &
the rhetoric of fools.

Parting Lovers, A Closing with Renewing Possibilities

Part One

There is more in the missing and the giving than in the
receiving. When love leaves, melody leaves, songs cease,
laughter becomes measured and brightens one's face less often.
Touch or being touched becomes highly discriminatory.
Certain touches are avoided. When love leaves,
a tearing takes place; it's like the center of one's heart being
ripped apart and exposed unfiltered
to sand or acid, like pollution. Sleeplessness
follows, one's inability to eat, and the sudden loss of weight is
inevitable for many. Others put on weight. The gaining
impacts the body: "junk food" and guilt
take the place of internal cleansing. When love is missing or
detained, there is a constant hit in the pit of the stomach,
simulating an indefinable emptiness. The loss of love is the
losing of a precious part, like being lost in action,
the mission other in you. For serious lovers,
for contemplative lovers, for lovers who understand the
silklike concentration of energy and spirit required, it will take
the noise and force of hurricanes, the lava of volcanoes, and
the disconnectedness of earthquakes to confirm the undoings
of this loveship. The quieting of this kind of love is not an
often occurrence, once in a generation, maybe twice in a
life-time. Such love is heart-rooted, sexually measured (hot),
thoughtfully shared, consistent, a slow and deliberate love
which will take the cultures and breathless thoughts of loving
others to demand its transition.

Part Two

Where end to end becomes beginning to beginning. The releasing of mind, soul, and spirit. The best cure for transitional love is to leave lovingly. To refocus and communicate, digest and internalize the crackings and earth-movings in your hearts. The ultimate healers for parting lovers is rest, is meditation, is re-evaluation of one's loveship. Healing requires waiting time, demands thinking time, needs liberating and insightful music. Healing is a sharing of pain with a trusted friend talking it out. More waiting time. Avoiding blame. Reconstructing of beautiful memories. Rebuilding thoughts. Conversations with one's self. Meditation. Deep study and creative productions. Exercise. Fasting. Cleansing. Cultural inner attainment. Surrounding one's self with nature and music, art, literature, dance; the quiet beat and rhythms of new life. Searching softly for the simple rejuvenative powers of nature. Reach for colors that are reflective. Search actively for certainty, smiles, and learned exactness of blooming new love. Take your time in the searching. Rising in this vast world are renewal possibilities. Spring, at planting time. New heat coming. Soon.

Part Three

If parting is necessary
part as lovers.
part as two people
who can still
smile & talk & share
the good & important
with each other.
part
wishing each other
happy
happy life
in a world
fighting against the
men and the women,
sisters and brothers
Black as
we.

Extended Families

*The extending of our families
has been our salvation.*

Voices with Loaded Language

For Bobbi Womack and Thelma Myers
December 26, 1993

you are not really friends to me
more like teachers, mothers, close nurturers,
i have listened to you for twenty-three years and
my enlargement has become quieted and determined
reflecting your words to me.

not quite stone,
you are more like rock-bone blended with flowers
of rainbow designing-black brownish-orange leaves
ordering up yellow suns
aiding your rising each morning
to strengthen our spines,
to make temporary treaties with tree-uprooters
bent on the annihilation of your off-spring,
the seasoning of your extended families.

you chose questions,
you quilted responsibility into my shoes,
your touch, darkly-soft, muted my anger
tuning it into focused toil,
permanent fruit. duty-deeds. resulting labor.
you are, as they say, "right on the dime," stone right.
I bring you flowers in the language of your teachings:
always consider your race positively,
contemplate deeply on your culture,
do not try to reason with sworn enemies.
be child centered in your family making,
be deliberate in your work.
meditate on bright tomorrows.
keep love central to your life.

Quality: Gwendolyn Brooks at 73
June 7, 1990

breath,
life after seven decades plus three years
is a lot of breathing. seventy three years on this
earth is a lot of taking in and giving out, is a
life of coming from somewhere and for many a bunch
of going nowhere.

how do we celebrate a poet who has created
music with words for over fifty years, who has
showered magic on her people, who has redefined
poetry into a black world exactness
thereby giving the universe an insight into
darkroads?

just say she interprets beauty and wants to
give life, say she is patient with phoniness
and doesn't mind people calling her gwen or sister.
say she sees the genius in our children, is visionary
about possibilities, sees as clearly as ray charles and
stevie wonder, hears like determined elephants looking
for food. say that her touch is fine wood, her memory
is like an african road map detailing adventure and
clarity, yet returning to chicago's south evans
to record the journey. say her voice is majestic
and magnetic as she speaks in poetry, rhythms, song
and spirited trumpets, say she is dark skinned,
melanin rich, small-boned, hurricane-willed,
with a mind like a tornado redefining the landscape.

life after seven decades plus three years
is a lot of breathing.
gwendolyn, gwen, sister g has
not disappointed our anticipations.
in the middle
of her eldership she brings us
vigorous language, memory,
illumination.

she brings breath.

Mothers

For Mittie Travis (1897–1989),
Maxine Graves Lee (1924–1959),
Inez Hall and Gwendolyn Brooks

"Mothers are not to be confused with
females who only birth babies"

mountains have less height
and
elephants less weight than
mothers who plan bright futures for their children
against the sewers of western life.

mothers making magical music miles from monster madness
are not news,
are not subject for doctorates.

how shall we celebrate mothers?
how shall we call them in the winter of their lives?
what melody will cure slow bones?
who will bring them worriless late-years?
who will thank them for hidden pains?

mothers are not broken-homes,
they are irreplaceable fire,
a kiss or smile at a critical juncture,
a hug or reprimand when doubts swim in,
a calm glance when the world seems impossible,
the back that america could not break.

mothers making magical music miles from monster madness
are not news,
are not subject for doctorates.

mothers instill questions and common sense,
urge mighty thoughts and lively expectations,
are impetus for discipline and intelligent work while
making childhood exciting, unforgettable and
        challenging.

mothers are preventative medicine
        they are
women who hold their children all night to break
        fevers,
women who cleaned other folks' homes in order to
        give their children homes,
women who listen when others laugh,
women who believe in their children's dreams,
women who lick the bruises of their children and
give up their food as they suffer hunger pains silently.

if mothers depart their precious spaces too early
values, traditions and bonding interiors are wounded,
morals confused, ethics unknown, needed examples
        absent and
crippling histories of other people's victories are
        passed on as knowledge.

mothers are not broken-homes,
they are gifts
sharing full hearts, friendships and mysteries.
as the legs of fathers are amputated
mothers double their giving
having seen the deadly future of white flowers.

mothers making magical music miles from monster madness
are not news,
are not subject for doctorates.

who will bring them juice in the sunset of their time?
who will celebrate the wisdom of their lives,
the centrality of their songs,
the quietness of their love,
the greatness of their dance?
it must be us,
able daughters, good sons
their cultural gift,
the fruits and vegetables of their medicine.

We must come like earthrich waterfalls.

Being Here

For Willie Green De Berry
(1913–1994)

this is our findings:
he knew how to carry water,
love a wife, rear children, crack nuts,
name a daughter after himself,
inquire about the friends of his children,
provide beans and beets, shoes, questions, safety &
       obstacles.
he was a tree.

his dying did not disable us
his creative preparation rooted our souls
providing not a living will but
a will to accept the life one has lived.
it is his sojourn that is remembered:
he was rock and bone, joy fed his heart,
they said he loved like a father,
his smiles and anger were tied to a greater good,
let's say he was blackman as anchor.
(in a land that did not allow him to be a captain)

he was our center
he lived the color green.

Too Many of our Young are Dying

moments represent a lifetime.

our hearts lose sunshine
when our children cease to smile words
and share with parents their passionate pain.
our children, in the millions,
are dropping from the trees of life too soon,
their innocent hearts & bodies
are forced to navigate within modern madness,
searching for life and love
in the basements of a crippled metropolis,
a disintegrating culture   too soon.

are we not all earth & lakes & sun?
are we not all mamas & babas to their young music?
their lives are not abstracted bragging rights,
we must never stop listening to their stories & songs.

when our children
do not share their young pain
it is a sign of our closed ears & punctured hearts
do not misread the silences in their eyes,
they are seeking sunshine from us
immediately.

Volcanoes in the Souls of Children

For Gwendolyn Calvert Baker
and the 1995 Chicago State University Graduates

we have learned to sleep on bare mattresses,
we measure our tomorrows against the deaths of
      eleven year olds
acculturated to the violence of Haiti, Somalia, Bosnia,
nonprescription rocks, and Stateway Gardens.*

why is self-hatred considered normal among us?
why are our children angry?
what motivates the failure fields in their eyes?
why, among strangers, is there raw passion in their
      hatred of us?

we refuse victimhood,
the depreciation of young minds is not to be rewarded!
only until we understand the offerings
can we appreciate rejection.

each decade there is a revisiting of Black intelligence.

it is not the logic that is repudiated in the rule of
'i' before 'e' except after 'c', it is the assertion of
teachers who believe that our learning rules of language is
      insignificant
in our speaking, writing, and understanding.
who are the measurers among us?
    who certified their knowledge?
    why do we have to beg and fight
    for that which others expect as normal nurturing?

* public housing on the South Side of Chicago

58

we reject victimhood,
great teachers discover their hearts early,
knowing that it is difficult to climb mountians without
visiting them.
practice brings permanency.
this is our calling. we are essential to each other's
crops. we are the rain, the sun, the deep dark, dark
soil renouncing the short life of concrete and the
cemented messages in its cracks. We are the bonded
meditative silence reading the future in each
other's eyes. celebrated vision. we are the yeses,
the can-dos, the give me a challenge-chance, the
mountains-builders, the quiet creators who understand
the innate children erupting earthwide and refusing
to be prey or martyr, repudiating foreign assessments.
first, belonging to each other, back-watchers.
quick minds dancing within the fire and mud. ready
for the wind. riding our own memories, history, future.

The Mission of a Good Man
For Robert J. Dale at Fifty

we must read this man differently
dark-skinned children are at the center of his heart.

he possesses a desperate joy,
few pleasures, easy laughter,
he takes time to hear
little voices.

his thoughts are reclusive, private, complex.
he lives among a community
that understands & calls his name often and
thinks that he is a mountain,
thinks that he is rice milk & precious stone.
they see him the way he sees our children.
honestly.

his interior is tree lined, African wheat grass,
   mountainous.
he has a suffering smile that understands
   voluminous truths.
he must make a payroll twice monthly,
         make deals with pants-wearing roaches with
         deep immune systems & bent smiles requiring him
         to bathe & meditate frequently. he says,
         for our children we must claim part of the map,
         geography is not european, is not white, must not
         be foreign to us.

we must receive this man accurately, traditionally.
dark-skinned children are at the heart of his center.
his heart is African.

All Children are Precious

For Barbara A. Sizemore
May 9, 1997

it is not uncommon to see her
in unexpected moments smiling at the loudly
    impossible.
the great mission in her life is measured
by making believers out of angry experts
who use toilet tissue to write their books and reports
on the largely impossible melodies,
they confirm noise, she hears music

strangers feel that her affection
is illegible but apparent.

her love is a Blackbold quilt
wearing the palm prints of children questioning
the direction of their fingers
the colors in their eyes and extreme ideas.
however, they are not opposing forces
their hearts are consumptive, calm and clear
when caring is present.

our children see the lies and failure in the eyes of
teachers who have given up.
our children survive cultural ignorance, soda pop,
potato chips and sweet cake breakfasts, each other
and people with earned degrees.
what are the ethics of children without self-knowledge?

she sees children as sacred places,
she has a repairable heart and
the quiet word on the street is that
Duke Ellington would have liked her smile.
in it gleams her greatest theme
the love of our children and the articulation of
their possibilities.

A Calling

For Rev. Frank Madison Reid III
on the occasion of 25 years of service in the ministry

we are short memory people,
too willing to settle for artless resumes of
rapid life   brief prayers cappuccino.

our young adapt to contemporary clothing without question,
as we fail to acknowledge brilliance among us
displaying a hesitancy to tell this preacherman, this
          good brother
how his journey has become our journey.
in him is ordered-calm, deep thought, quality-love, a
probing mind.

are pastors inspired to read Baldwin, Morrision, Diop,
Chomsky, Said and Brooks? are their ears prepared for Monk,
Aretha, Trane, Chuck D and music screaming for the tongues
of hypocrites? can a serious minister be known for anything
other than knowing God's name, being clean, loving his family
and saying double yes to fried chicken dinners? cultural
essentiality?

we are short-memory people,
you have been planted among us
artfully seeded in Black earth to illuminate the texts,
shepherd our prayers, spiritualize our commitments and help
us heal the holes in our souls.

some arrogantly shout that this is your job,
in kind smiles and rather meditatively, others voice
we don't remember you ever filling out an
          employment application.

Why You are Here

For Clifford Watson
February 8, 1998

We are cut from the same tree
not logs, scraps of wood or toothpicks
but
molded as sculptured future by rock cutters
translating their art on to the roots
of long life, baobab trees having
endured the hurricanes, volcanoes and
earthquakes of
sprinting in America.

Our lives have never been at peace.

You have communities that love you.
We do not say it often enough.
With nourishment of millet and lentils
you have been our tall structure
an eloquent fire, sacred and on course.
We now keep each other's scrapbooks and smiles.

The State's Answer to Economic Development

it is the poor
that populate Las Vegas & riverboat casinos
where neon lights & one-armed bandits never die
yet draw the young
& aged whose lives
seem exhausted & bored beside
the lights,
the games,
the entertainment,
the unchances,
the early hope
where everybody can afford
a hotel room to drop a suitcase
with fresh greyhound tags notating
the midnight ride from California & elsewhere
with $300 in their left shoes
that they think
will win them a life.

The B Network

brothers bop & pop & be-bop in cities locked up
and chained insane by crack and other acts
of desperation computerized in pentagon cellars
          producing
boppin brothers boastin of being better,
          best & beautiful.

if the boppin brothers are beautiful where are the sisters
who seek brotherman with a drugless head unbossed or beaten
by the bodacious West?

in a time of big wind being blown by boastful brothers,
will other brothers beat back backwardness to better & best
without braggart bosses beatin butts,
takin names and diggin graves?

beatin badness into bad may be urban but is it beautiful
          & serious?
or is it betrayal in an era of prepared easy death hangin
          on corners
trappin young brothers before they know the difference
          between big death and big life?

brothers bop and pop and be-bop in cities locked up
and chained insane by crack and other acts
of desperation computerized in pentagon cellars producing
boppin brothers boastin of being better, best, beautiful &
definitely not *Black*.

the critical best is that brothers
better be the best if they are to avoid backwardness
brothers better be the best if they are to conquer
        beautiful bigness
comprehend that bad is only *bad* if it's big, black and better
        than boastful braggarts belittling our best and brightest
with bosses seeking inches when miles are better.

brothers need to bop to being Black & bright &
        above board
the black train of beautiful wisdom that is bending this bind
toward a new & knowledgeable beginning that is
bountiful & bountiful & beautiful
while be-bopin to be
better than the test,
brotherman.

better yet write the exam.

jimmy lee

jimmy lee is my dad,
my mothers told me so
my birth certificate states it,
his mother, my grandmother confirms that he is,
my aunt, his half-sister swears it to be,
my sister, his daughter believes it to be true.

on the street i am known as the son of mr. lee.
i have his height, artistic bent, independent spirit,
love of music, size 11 1/2 feet and an
uncanny ability to spot and tell a lie quicker than a
fastball taking on speed toward a rookie at
bat for the very first time.

jimmy lee is my dad,
he calls me son whenever he wants something,
this is the only evidence that i have of his fatherhood,
it has been a profound lesson and
i have never liked baseball.

Courage

For Betty Shabazz (1936–1997)

how does one proceed with half a heart?
what is the message in this transition from
body to spirit to the quiet recesses of our minds,
what should we take from this passing?

there are people who think that their lives are *the* truth.
we walk blindly in the city and the city is all we know
as ignorant people talk about how ignorant other
   people are,
this woman would smile with extended hand and
   heart,
her soul had experienced the white night of loss.

the culturally honest and spiritual among us
are always lied to and laughed at.
in their loneliness they seldom speak
we do not understand them.
we fear their peace and presence,
we fear their questioning the lies in us,
we fear their liberation.

courage is not leaving the battle until the last child is
        accounted for,
courage is saying no to the gossip of fools, friends and foe,
courage is examining the laws and souls of sworn enemies,
courage is creating a life of good values, kindness and small
        deeds,
courage is this woman, Betty Shabazz, daring to cross
     the crack in the concrete
drawn by dull-witted prophets who
mistrust the truth of their own god.

Brad

For Walter Bradford (1937–1997)

We met during the explosive decade of the sixties. Both of us
were on fire. Young and ready to attack evil as we knew it.
Both of us experienced the military at the end of our teen
years, which prepared us to be impatient around children with
guns and boys in black playing military. We kept our criticism
to ourselves because we were still young, full of hope and
energy and robust tomorrows.

We were poor and extremely grateful for Chicago's community
colleges—a place where we first met and encountered the
challenge of structured intellectual life.

Gwendolyn Brooks, Hoyt W. Fuller and the brothers and
sisters of OBAC* carried our voices. Their workshops helped
us to refine our narratives. Writing poetry was to be our way
out. We had fire-words to share with each other and the
world. And, somehow we knew that we would make a differ-
ence.

You made a difference. There are hundreds of men and
women who knew you by "Brad" and they too realized that
you were exceptional and on loan to us. You could organize a
Chinese puzzle and make sense out of Black people born into
fear, bondage, confusion and a European system that negated
their very souls. Your chocolate smile will be missed and I'm
not alone in my sadness.

* Organization of Black American Culture

This Poet: Gwendolyn Brooks at Eighty
June 6, 1997

this poet, this genuine visionary,
this carrier of the human spirit,
this chronicler of the Blackside of life,
this kind and gentle person is the reason
we lend our voices to this day.

that other poets have championed good writing
and literature, have exposed evil
in the world, have contributed mightily of personal resources
to the young, to the would-be-writers,
to students and to the institutions of common good
is without a doubt. however,
the only poet who has made it a mission
to incorporate all of this and more into a wonderful and
dedicated lifestyle is Gwendolyn Brooks.

without press releases, P.R. people or interpreters
from the academy the great work of this quiet poet
has touched a city, this state, our nation and the world.
her poetry, her childrens books,
her essays and her autobiographies have given us an insight
into the complexities of the Black human condition
that few writers can match, yet we all try
she *is* our standard.
seventy years of writing do make a difference.

we gratefully and gracefully walk in her shadow,
not because she needs or requests that we do so;
it is that her work,
her outstanding contribution to Black literary music
in this world that demands the best from the least of us.
at eighty she needs no introductions or encouraging words.
at eighty the notes she writes to herself
are more comprehensive and in larger letters.

at eighty her walk is slower and her eyesight less certain.
at eighty she loves silence, is never voiceless or alone,
at eighty, Blackness remains her star and
she alerts her readers always to the huge possibility
of knowing ones self, others,
and the mystery and joy of a full life.

she has approached 320 seasons
on her own terms.
she has taken the alphabet and structured a language.
she has walked thousands of miles carrying her own baggage.

she has done the work she aimed to do,
children call her "Mama Gwen" and memorize her lines.

that which is "incomplete" is at her home
on the dining room table, in neat piles
enclosed in all size packages,
open and unopened,
here and only here is where she will always be behind

she is the last of the great
handwritten letter answerers and
she will not be able to keep up with this volume of
love.

Etta

For Etta Moten Barnett at 96

Etta, not accepting exclusion or
the concept *can't* leaped creatively and courageously into the
20th century. her talent, eloquent and grand evoked
sun, moon, boiling water and 12 grain bread. Solid
she was known to harbor mountains in her heart,
her prodigous artistry conquered the agnosticisms of
minute-minded women and smiling men as lessor souls
buck-danced to the promises of colored stardom. Soon.
Etta at ninety-six is our clear memorandum,
an endearing spirit who took her dreams and songs,
her dance and drama and gracefully grounded a
cultural signature on three generations and a continent.
Solid. as she is.

if you lose your optimism
you're in serious trouble
For Leon Forrest (1937–1997)

i never knew the
coal that burned dark between us.
i understood your reinvented fire.
appreciated the dance, music and optimism in you.
recognized the writer, lover, professor running in you.
quietly this evening
i wished we had had winter-fights
lengthy talks, small arguments or deafening
disagreements stretching into the night of our imaginations.
i'll miss those nonconversations between novelist and poet.
i'll think of you while thanking you as i and others
continue our majestic journey
paging through the inspiring puzzles and prizes
of your language.

So Many Books, So Little Time
For librarians & independent booksellers

Frequently during my mornings of pain & reflection
when I can't write
or articulate my thoughts
or locate the mindmusic needed
to complete the poems & essays
that are weeks plus days overdue
forcing me to stop, I say, cease
answering my phone, eating right, running my miles,
reading my mail and making love.
(Also, this is when my children do not seek me out
because I do not seek them out)
I escape north to the nearest library or used bookstore.
They are my retreats, my quiet energy/givers, my
       intellectual refuge.

For me it is not bluewater beaches, theme parks
or silent chapels hidden among forest greens.
Not multistored American malls, corporate book
supermarkets, mountain trails or Caribbean hideaways.

My sanctuaries are liberated lighthouses of shelved books,
featuring forgotten poets, unread anthropologists &
playwrights; starring careful anthologists of art & photography.
upstart literary critics; introducing dissertations of
tenure-seeking, assistant professors, self-published geniuses,
remaindered first novelists; highlighting speed-written best-
sellers, wise historians & theologians, nobel & pulitzer prize
winning poets & fiction writers, overcertain political
       commentators,
small press wonderkinds & learned academics.
All are vitamins for my slow brain & sidetracked spirit in this
winter of creating.

I do not believe in smiling politicians, AMA doctors,
zebra-faced bankers, red-jacketed real estate or
automobile salespeople or singing preachers.

I believe in books.
it can be conveniently argued that knowledge,
not that which is condensed or computer packaged, but
pages of hard-fought words, dancing language
meticulously & contemplatively written by the likes of
        me & others,
shelved imperfectly at the levels of open hearts & minds
is preventive medicine strengthening me for the return to my
clear pages of incomplete ideas to be reworked, revised &
written as new worlds and words in all of their subjective
configurations, eventually to be processed into books that will
hopefully be placed on the shelves of libraries & bookstores to
be found & browsed over by receptive booklovers,
readers & writers looking for a retreat,
looking for departure & home,
looking for open heart surgery without the knife.

Grandfathers: They Speak Through Me

For W.E.B. Du Bois and Paul Robeson

His father's father prepared him to bite his tongue,
power-listening became his gateway to information
and race knowledge.
his mother's father embraced him fully with large hugs and
words of "can-do" possibilities
in a time of darkness and treachery.
I was their blood mixture, their bone,
their claim to immortality and song.

grandfather graves declared white
people deficient, diseased and dangerous,
he had scars documenting it, he,
an african-black laborer could fix anything
moving that had a motor, a self-taught mechanic
who was gang beaten at 22 for correcting a white man at a
chevy dealership at a time when the accepted
attitude in arkansas for negroes in the presence
of whites was head bowed, eyes deep to the ground. quiet.
defeated.

grandfather lee a bronze colored
detroit minister of the baptist persuasion
never worked a day for white folks, god talked to him early
and he kept his smile.
he pastored to a community where eyes and work seldom said
no or "can't do," starting from a store front, growing into a
used movie theater, to building from the earth up,
into a 1,500 seat stained glass, concrete and fine wood
cathedral, this became an answer.
god was his mission, his people his melody
and neither *quit* nor *quiet* were in him.
he anchored bronzeville, negotiated with white stones, had
what his congregation called good back-up, the solid feed of
osun, obatala and shango.

at six i was at their knees consuming words, jerks,
silences and secrets.
at eleven i was taken to the woods and left with knife, water
and a map, manhood was coming. soon.
at thirteen i was taken to the pulpit,
given the bible, songbook and silver watch,
jesus was in the air and always on time.
at fourteen i discovered richard wright, louis
armstrong, chester himes, miles davis, langston hughes,
gwendolyn brooks and motown. i was branded crazy, insolent
and world-wounded for the questions i asked and for the
burn in my eyes.
as a young man i carried many knowledges,
ran between two cultures,
cleared my head in the military and libraries
and cried for the loss of my mother.
i kissed girls and black politics on the g.i. bill in college and
was exiled into black struggle in the early sixties.
i learned to ride the winds of battle.

as a man i choose poetry, love and extended family.
i selected black independence, institution building and
the cheery eyes of children as my mission.
i breathe the smoke and oxygen from the fires of my
        grandfathers,
i have their slow smile, quick mind and necessary wit, i wear
their earth shoes and dance with their languages,

i speak in the cadences of southern trees,
holy water and books,
i carry their messages and courageous hearts,
my eyes are ancestor deep, bold and intrepid,
i whisper their songs as mantras.
my music is accelerated blues, the four tops and trane.
it is they, my grandfathers who taught me the notes and
rhythms and as the son of their sons
i'm not missing a beat.

You Will Recognize Your Brothers

You will recognize your brothers
by the way they act and move throughout the world.
there will be a strange force about them,
there will be unspoken answers in them.
this will be obvious not only to you but to many.
the confidence they have in themselves and in
their people will be evident in their quiet saneness.
the way they relate to women will be
clean, complimentary, responsible,
with honesty and as partners.
the way they relate to children will be
strong and soft full of positive direction and as example.
the way they relate to men
will be that of questioning our position in this world,
will be one of planning for movement and change,
will be one of working for their people,
will be one of gaining and maintaining trust within the culture.
these men at first will seem strange and unusual but
this will not be the case for long.
they will train others and the discipline they display
will be a way of life for many.
they know that this is difficult
but this is the life that they have chosen
for themselves, for us, for life:
they will be the examples,
they will be the answers, they will be the first line builders,
they will be the creators,
they will be the first to give up the weakening pleasures,
they will be the first to share love, resources and vision,
they will be the workers,
they will be the scholars,
they will be the providers,
they will be the historians,

they will be the doctors, lawyers, farmers, priests
and all that is needed for development and growth.
you will recognize these brothers
and
they will not betray you.

Books as Answer

In recognition of National Black Book Week
(February 23–March 1)

there was only one book in our home
it was briefly read on sundays and
in between the lies & promises of smiling men
who slept with their palms out & pants unzipped.
it was known by us children as *the* sunday book.

rain and books & sun and books to read
in a home where books were as strange as
money and foreign policy discussions
and I alone searched for meaning
where rocks & belts & human storms
disguised themselves as answers, reference and revelation.
and I a young map of what is missing and wrong
in a home empty of books, void of liberating
words dancing as poetry and song,
vacuous of language that reveals pictures of
one's own fields, spirits, cities and defining ideas.
and I without the quiet contemplation that meditative prose
      demands,
was left free to drink from the garbage cans of riotous
      imaginations,
was sucked into the poverty of cultural destruction & violent
      answers.

until
someone, a stranger, a dark skinned woman with natural hair,
in a storefront library laid a book in front of me
and the language looked like me, walked like me,
talked to me, pulled me into its rhythms & stares,
slapped me warmly into its consciousness and read,

rain and books & sun and books,
we are each other's words & winds
we are each other's breath & smiles,
we are each other's memories & mores,
we build our stories page by page
chapter by chapter, poem by poem, & play by play
to create a life, family, culture, & a civilization
where it will take more than sixty seconds
to tell strangers who you really are,
to tell enemies and lovers your name.

Rwanda: Where Tears Have No Power

Who has the moral high ground?

Fifteen blocks from the whitehouse
on small corners in northwest, d.c.
boys disguised as men rip each other's hearts out
with weapons made in china. they fight for territory.

across the planet in a land where civilization was born
the boys of d.c. know nothing about their distant relatives
in rwanda. they have never heard of the hutu or tutsi people.
their eyes draw blanks at the mention of kigali, byumba
or butare. all they know are the streets of d.c., and do not
cry at funerals anymore. numbers and frequency have a way
of making murder commonplace and not news
unless it spreads outside of our house, block, territory.

modern massacres are intraethnic. bosnia, sri lanka, burundi,
nagorno-karabakh, iraq, laos, angola, liberia and rwanda are
small foreign names on a map made in europe. when bodies
by the tens of thousands float down a river turning the water
the color of blood, as a quarter of a million people flee barefoot
into tanzania and zaire, somehow we notice. we do not smile,
we have no more tears. we hold our thoughts. In deeply
muted silence looking south and thinking that today
nelson mandela seems much larger
than he is.

Haiti

For the Haitian people and Randall Robinson

in haiti at wahoo bay beach of port-au-prince
there are beautiful women in bathing suits
with men who are young, light-skinned and rich.
you are welcomed if you run with the right wolves.

in port-au-prince, on the other side of the water
fenced off from wahoo bay beach
a few children receive 19th century education in
one room shanties without running water or toilets.
their parents cook on outdoor woodfires and
pass waste in secret spots or community latrines.
they live in poverty within poverty and they elected a   priest
to represent their dreams.
he promised food, clean water, education, wood, seeds,
            fairness, democracy and peace on earth.

the people of haiti are angry with u.s. presidents.
the haitian military forced their elected priest to flee in the
night, with their dreams and prayers
in a quickly packed suitcase.

the people are uneducated, not stupid.
democracy is coming to south africa and
haiti drowns in white promises.
bill clinton talks in codes as
paramilitary terror squads beat patriotism into the people.
american businesses pay 14 cents an hour to the peasants
and
provide japanese toys and airline tickets to the elite.

the people of haiti are angry with u.s. presidents.
they take boat rides by the thousands
to cross a sea made of their dead for america.
most are returned on military ships,

unsuitable as political refugees.
we are told that race is not the problem
it is the island, its not cuba.

the rich in haiti diet,
the poor starve and disappear if they complain too loudly.
randall robinson lived on water and tomato juice
his eyes sank into his forehead for a month.
his eyes are clear and so is he.

the new duvalierists rule a dirty capital,
when rain comes the people join the mud,
the rich drive jeeps made in the U.S.A.
the "MREs"—morally repugnant elite—are like elite
everywhere:
they do not feel for others,
they hide their eyes,
they wear foreign made clothes,
their children have private playgrounds and education,
they live on hills and laugh at the dark people who don't
even own the night.
they speak the language of killers.

the rich do not fear elected priests or ignorant peasants,
they have good uncles across the water,
currently he is grayish blond,
has a smooth southern accent,
and talks real fast from both sides of his mouth
before him
a transplanted texan played cowboy on the high seas
before him
a californian with an excellent make-up man
yawned whenever haiti was mentioned
before him...

Peace Starts Inside You

smile. breathe deeply, inhale. hold. exhale.
envy no one erase jealousy from your mind, heart &
words. speak & think good of self & others. awaken
the life spirit inside of you. breathe deeply the good in
you. smile. seek wholeness & calm. breathe.
plant good thoughts of peace & knowledge. smile often
as you breathe forgiveness and reciprocity. search
the silence in you that releases the noise that contains
the grays, whites, plastic and clocks blocking the
life force in your morning stretches. slowly breathe & smile.
breathe away ignorance, revenge, incompetence & mediocrity.
work your inner-self. breathe & smile life into your cells.
eliminate corrupt thoughts, words & actions. study peace.
smile. breathe yes into your life, to love. to family.
       to happiness. to children & children & children
       becoming the reflection of you.
discover stillness. vegetation. water. earth. breathe. health. joy.
smile. silence. breathe deeply, inhale. hold. exhale. smile. life
stillness. smile for good work, deep study, wellness.
quiet consciousness
calm within the quiet,
peace be still.
smile & breathe
release. relief.

in writing, in creating and
creation
using words to make pictures and portraits
there is always an end
and a time to say
thanks;
find yourself here among
the many and
the *One*.
Peace and Love.